Power of Prayer
and
Scriptural Healing

May you be blessed and empowered by God
as you read this book on the
"Power of Prayer and Scriptural Healing."
Remember to "Pray without ceasing"
1 Thess. 5:17
God Bless

Min. Patricia G. Williams *P. Wne*

5/3/14

Power of Prayer
and
Scriptural Healing

(A Devotional Spiritual Journey)

Patricia Gabriel Williams

To order additional copies of this book, contact:
Xlibris LLC
1-888-795-4274
www.Xlibris.com
Orders@Xlibris.com
548131

CONTENTS

ACKNOWLEDGEMENTS

This book is written first of all to honor my Lord and Savior Jesus Christ who has been with me throughout my journey through illness and healing. I dedicate this book to three people who have greatly influenced my life for the Lord. I must first dedicate this book in memory of my loving husband, Pastor Lucius Williams Jr., of thirty-nine years, who recently passed away. He was truly a gift from God who encouraged me in all areas of life to be the best I could for the Lord. He has always encouraged me to complete this book.

Secondly, this book is a tribute to the loving memory of my mother, Mrs. Tiney Louise Gabriel, who showed me a great example of a "Praying mother". When I was a child I saw my mother spend so much time on her knees praying that she would sometimes fall asleep and wake up and continue to pray. I remember some experiences of praying with her and how she prayed about everything and everybody she could remember. This spirit of prayer and praise has entered my life and I am now a praying mother and grandmother. I can not say that I pray as long as my mother did, but I pray with the same strength and power that comes from almighty God. The third person I want to dedicate this book to in loving memory is my niece, Alchan

Patricia Miller, who passed away from complications from Lupus. She was a great encouragement to the entire family because of her love and joy in life in spite of health conditions. She saw my love for the Lord and said she wanted to be an Evangelist like me, even before I was called into the ministry. Out of gratitude to God for all He has done for me and my family, a portion of the book sales will be donated to the APM (Alchan P. Miller) Memorial Fund for Lupus Research.

I would like to thank the many people who prayed for me and who called and gave encouragement and have waited patiently during the long process of writing and getting this book published. Two special people who prayed for me were Elder and Sis. Richardson of the Forerunners Of Christ Ministries. Sis. Richardson shared a long list of scriptures on healing which became a part of my daily reading during my illness. Eventually, these Scriptures became a part of the list of Scriptures in this book.

My daughter Desiree was a tremendous help in typing the initial Scriptures for the book. A special thanks to my sister, Bettie Miller and her family who have been there with encouragement and support throughout my life.

Pastor Rebecca Simmons has taken on the challenge my husband gave her to encourage me to get this book published. Her persistence in following up, editing and carrying forth and encouraging me to finish this book is greatly appreciated. It may have taken a lot longer without her help. I can not thank her enough for letting God use her.

INTRODUCTION

I must start out by saying that I never thought I would be writing a book on healing because I felt I did not know enough about the subject. I knew I would one day write a book, but I thought that my first book would be in Christian Education since I enjoyed the subject and had been trained in that area of study. Little did I know that the Holy Spirit was prompting me, after my last surgery, to go on a journey in healing and wholeness that resulted in the writing of this book.

I have gone through several surgeries, and God was dealing with me and asking me, "What have you *learned about me* that you can *share* with someone else *who is hurting*? Something that will help them know me better and will enhance your knowledge of me?"

This book is written out of *joy* as well as *sorrow*; the joy of knowing that Jesus has been with me through every struggle, every pain and every healing. He has been my joy in the midst of all the sorrows and defeats. I have *learned to depend on His Word* through it all. I have read these Scriptures on healing throughout my last journey in healing. I have also read these Scriptures with my husband as he recovered from quadruple bi-pass open heart surgery. And finally, I read them through my mother's journey after brain tumor surgery. I have shared the Scripture portion of this book with many who were sick. They have encouraged me to finish this book because it helped so much in their recovery.

Reading the Word of God daily during my mother's illness helped encourage her as well as myself. Even though my mother developed complications and consequently passed away two months after the surgery, she had joy and peace throughout her ordeal. Many days she would raise her arm in the air to give God praise. At first, I thought she was in pain when she held her arm up in the air because she was not able to communicate in words. But one night I was listening to a preacher and found myself lifting my arm high in the air out of praise to God. That's when the Spirit of God made me aware of what she was doing. My mother knew the Lord as her Savior and was a faithful prayer warrior through prayer and actions of love.

Even though my mother passed from her earthly existence, she went on to be with God where she would receive her total healing and deliverance.

Personally, these Scriptures were a source of strength for me as I went through surgery for a malignant tumor and subsequent treatments. As I went through one of the most difficult periods in my life of sickness and pain of suffering, I was daily reminded by the Word of God of His divine presence. In Ephesians 3:20, it states that God is able to do exceedingly and abundantly above all that we ask or think according to His power that works within us. I knew I was never alone; not because I had a loving and supportive husband, daughter, and family, but because God said He would never leave me nor forsake me. When you are going through sickness, depression, pain or agony, no physical person can comfort you like the love of God can. You need that spiritual love that reaches down deep in your soul. Each day God leads me to read the Scriptures and give Him praise before and after reading the Word.

The Lord impressed on my heart to tape myself as I read the Word daily and gave God praise. This tape served as comfort day by day. The Scripture, Hebrews 11:1, which states, *"Now faith is the substance of things hoped for, the evidence of things not seen,"* was a constant source of strength for me. The Word began as the Scripture says to *"take on flesh"* and dwell within me during some long nights of illness. I could feel God's soothing, healing power as I listened to the Word and gave God praise. My belief in what God could do increased within me. Each day, as I experienced God's healing power in my body I began to feel better spiritually, physically, mentally and emotionally. No one can tell me that God does not still heal today! I know God raised me up and gave me another chance at life.

HEALING
THROUGH PHYSICAL DIET

One thing I realized was that my diet was tied into my sickness. My immune system was not strong enough to survive the disease that attacked my body. Something had to be done if I wanted to live a productive life. I discovered that my diet was more a part of my sickness than I had imagined. The malignant tumor that I was diagnosed with had caused me to examine my lifestyle. My diet, as well as my hectic schedule which included trying to balance our church ministry, family obligations, and a business, had caused my body systems to weaken.

I had been plagued for many years with little tumors that indicated that something was wrong with my health, and it was time to take charge of my life. I prayed, and God directed me to the help I needed. I was directed to a friend who was a nurse and was made aware of a seminar dealing with health and wholeness.

Little did I know that attending this seminar was one of the best decisions I could have made. In the seminar, the value of eating more vegetables and fruits as a part of your diet was stressed. Yes, I knew that vegetables and fruits were good for the body, but I was not thinking that this would be a source of needed nutrients for my healing. They also stressed eating little or no meat, and becoming a vegetarian. Well, I can not say that I stopped eating meat, but I did limit my intake. During the time of my illness, I went on a mostly vegetable and fruit diet. I started juicing my vegetables. I made a daily energy drink in which I used a five pound bag of fresh carrots, along with two stalks of celery, an apple and a small portion of parsley. These ingredients were juiced together to make my daily drink.

This sixteen ounce vegetable and fruit drink twice a day served as the basic food in my diet during the time of my chemo treatments, which were rough on my body's system. I also ate other fruits and vegetables, and small portions of chicken, fish, and turkey. Vitamins were also a part of my personal daily regiment. I took 100 mg. of B6, Vitamin E at 400 mg, and a garlic tablet as my source of energy. God really strengthened me during this time. Most of the time, I felt well enough to continue with my regular daily activities. I thank God that I did not have to miss church too much during my recovery time. I looked forward to being in the midst of worship, prayer and praise. Church attendance with saints added support and strength during my time of healing.

During this time I met with a nutritionist who introduced me to other products including supplements by the Aim Company called "Trio" which included Barley Green, Just Carrots and Beets in a powdered form. This mixture made a pleasant tasting drink packed with vitamins and minerals. I no longer had to juice all of those pounds of carrots each day. This was really a blessing for it saved me a lot of time and energy.

After the treatment process was over, I have continued on these products because they give me extra strength. I have also become a representative for the Aim Company so I can share these and other products with people who might need them. In order for you to experience total healing, it will be necessary for you to change your diet.

An important element of your new diet is to drink plenty of water. At least six to eight glasses of distilled water is recommended per day. Some sources say that spring or purified water is just as good, but my nutritionist stressed distilled water. Please do some prayerful research for yourself. It is always good to check with your doctor if you are on certain medications because everyone's body is different. I am still struggling with keeping consistent in drinking the required amount of water each day and making time for exercise, but I know they are needed for my body's health.

Daily exercise of some sort is good whether it be walking, jogging, bike riding, the treadmill, or your own routine of exercises. As I began to exercise each day, I began to experience the blessings of God in my health and strength. I thank God for restoring my health. I am only taking one medication now for hypertension, and I believe God is going to heal me from even this condition.

Addressing the health issue is a very important part of *staying well for God's service*. We tend to get so busy with work, church, family and other responsibilities that our physical health is put on the back seat of our lives.

God is always to be first, and our personal health should be a part of the priorities of our lives. 1 Corinthians 6:19 states the following, *"Know ye not that your body is the temple of the Holy Ghost which is in you, which ye have of God, and ye are not your own?"*

I learned much about stress and anxiety in my career as a college counselor and psychology teacher for thirteen years. My students were taught the meaning of these terms in class, but life taught them and me much more about what the pressures and struggles of life can produce in us.

I had a very busy schedule *counseling, teaching and working on various committees* at the college and in the community. This did not include the *church ministry, family obligations, and responsibilities* which also demanded some more of my time. It was during this time that I first started to have signs of stress-related illnesses. My neck would become so sore and painful that I would have to rest a few days to recover. It was during that time that I had frequent colds and eventually small tumors began to appear in my body. Only a few times were the tumors serious enough to require treatment, but they were a sign that something was going wrong inside.

In looking back over my life, I found that even though I enjoyed working at my career and church ministry, they had begun to take a toll on my health. The lack of proper rest, a balanced diet, and exercise can cause all kinds of health issues.

When I went through these times I would stop and adjust my life style for a season or two, but eventually, other projects at work and ministry would take priority again. I have to continuously seek God's wisdom about my health even today to keep my life paced for God's will and not my own.

I find that if our lives are filled with continuous stress and anxiety, then we need to take time off to reduce some of the stressfulness in our lives. It is important to take a mini vacation if possible or even a day off occasionally to rewind and regroup our thoughts with the Lord. Sometimes just doing something different that God is leading you to do will help the situation.

Philippians 4:6 states "Be anxious for nothing but with prayer, and supplication and thanksgiving make your request known unto God." This Scripture seems to help me when I feel over burdened with issues. God is the real source of stress removal from our lives! Remember to work on your health, but do not forget to use the *Word of God* as your source of *strength* and *power.*

PRAYER, PURPOSE AND POWER

You have heard it said that you need to pray. Some may ask, *"Why do we need to pray?"* And others may say, *"I really do not know how to pray?"* or *"What is prayer anyway?"* Prayer is one of the greatest acts of the Christian believer. Prayer is talking to God and God talking back to you. It is a conversation with our all-powerful and loving God. It is having fellowship with God. It is not enough to just have knowledge of God, but we must spend time in prayer with God. Being alone with God and meditating on the Word of God in prayer is very important. For prayer to be effective, we must put our whole attention on God. Who would want to have a relationship with someone that spends little or no time with them? Anyone you truly love, you will want to spend time with them. We must love God with all our heart, mind, body, and soul. Prayer is the greatest secret weapon that believers have. It is as natural as breathing. It is as necessary as the air we breathe.

In praying, you must surrender to God. You may say, "What am I surrendering to God?" You must surrender yourself and your time. These are two precious assets to you and to God. As you pray, you begin to submit your will and your ways to God. In this act of submission, you will experience your prayers being heard and answered by

17

God. Some answers are immediate with a yes or no. But some answers we have to wait patiently for God to give them. The Scripture in Isaiah 40:31 states that "they that wait upon the Lord shall renew their strength; they shall mount up with wings like an eagle; they shall run and not get weary; and they shall walk and not faint."

You may wonder how you can hear God's answer. The more you pray and read God's Word, the more you will know God's voice when He speaks to your spirit. The Scripture states that "My sheep hear my voice and know and follow me." (John 10:27). If you seek to know God better, you will hear His voice even more clearly. For if we will acknowledge God in all our ways He will direct our paths (Proverbs 3:6).

Some things can hinder God's answer to your prayers. First of all, according to Scriptures in Romans 10:9-10, you must confess your sins and accept Jesus Christ as Lord and Savior. If you have not taken this important step for your healing and deliverance, you need to stop now and do this. For we need to be forgiven of our sins and be cleansed from all unrighteousness. In 1 John 1:9, it states that if we confess our sins he is faithful to forgive our sins and cleanse us from all unrighteousness.

Some of us fear getting too close to God because we feel we will have to give up too much in our lives. The truth is that any thing that you have to give up, God will help you do it. You do not have to do anything in your own strength. The Scripture says you can do all things through Christ who strengthens you. Others feel that God will get in their business. God already knows all things and does all things well. He is concerned about every area of our lives. He's in our business twenty four hours a day, seven days a week. He is in every aspect and every little detail. He is in our Myspace.com, Facebook, cell phone conversations, and all our private conversations. He is even in the intimate details in our personal relationships, in our home, our bedroom, and our bed. So, we might as well admit our faults and failures and move on in our growth in God. For God has said He will never leave us or forsake us. We will need

God's comforting Spirit as we go through many dark hours in our lives.

When we pray, we also request things from the Lord. We can trust God to meet our every need. We must believe when we pray that God hears us and will answer our prayers. His answers may be yes, no, or wait. He does not always answer when we first ask, but His answer will always be on time, every time He answers. If we read in Matthew 6:5-13, God gives some instruction on how to pray. A good way to begin our prayer is with "Our Father which art in Heaven." Then we can begin to ask for forgiveness. Once you have established God's forgiveness in your life and began your relationship with Him, you are ready to move on to receive total healing! Let's begin your journey of healing through 15 days of Scripture, prayer and daily devotional reflections.

15 DAYS

TO

SCRIPTURAL HEALING

DAY 1

PRAYER

These are sample prayers that I prayed before beginning my Scripture reading in the morning and evening. Feel free to use these during your 15 days of scriptural healing or write your own prayers as you are led by the Lord.

Morning Prayer

Dear Heavenly Father, As I come before you this morning knowing that you are a holy, loving, and all powerful God. I give you praise, honor, and glory for all you are doing in my life. Lord, I ask you for forgiveness of all my sins and that you will cleanse me from all unrighteousness. I thank you for keeping me through the night and allowing me to see a new day.

Lord, I submit myself, my family, and others today for your healing and whatever blessings we may need this day. Prepare my heart, mind, body, and soul to receive your Word today. I pray this prayer in Jesus' name. Amen.

Evening Prayer

Dear God, as I come before you at the close of another day, I have joy knowing that your love keeps me throughout the day. It gives me peace that you are all-knowing, all-powerful, and everywhere at once God. I can be assured that there is nothing going on down here that you do not know about and that you can not stop. I confess that some days I am tempted to doubt what you can do when I look at my circumstances. But, that doubt immediately fades away when I meditate on what you promised and what you have already done for me in my lifetime.

I thank you and praise you for this day, as I submit my fears, my anxieties, my questions and concerns to you. I know you care about what hurts me or disturbs my spirit and will answer my prayers in due season. Please open your Word to me through the Scriptures and give me strength to overcome.

This prayer I pray in the precious name of Jesus. Amen.

Write Your Own Prayers (Only if you wish to use your own personal prayers.)

Personal Morning Prayer

_____
_____
_____
_____
_____
_____
_____
_____
_____
_____
_____

Personal Evening Prayer

_____
_____
_____
_____
_____
_____
_____
_____
_____
_____
_____
_____
_____
_____

SCRIPTURE MEDITATION

Exodus 15:26 And said, if thou wilt diligently hearken to the voice of the Lord thy God, and wilt do that which is right in his sight, and wilt give ear to his commandment and keep all his statutes, I will put none of these diseases upon thee, which I have brought upon the Egyptians: for I am the Lord that healeth thee.

Exodus 23:25 And ye shall serve the Lord your God, and he shall bless thy bread, and thy water, and I will take sickness away from the midst of thee.

Deuteronomy 7:14-15 Thou shalt be blessed above all people: there shall not be male or female barren among you, or among your cattle. And the Lord will take away from thee all sickness, and will put none of the evil diseases of Egypt, which thou knowest upon thee; but will lay them upon all them that hate thee.

DAILY DEVOTIONAL REFLECTIONS DAY 1

Take God At His Word

As we begin our journey by faith into healing, one thing we must learn is that we must take God at His Word. For God said in Exodus 15:26 that we must listen to and obey His Word and do that which is right in His sight. As a result, God will keep the diseases of the flesh and spirit off of us. God is so faithful. He will even cause our physical food to be blessed. The food will preserve health and provide ingredients needed for healing in our body, mind and soul. None of these diseases can any longer live in our bodies and health will spring forth in us.

It is very important to confess our sins daily and get in line with the Word of God so that we may not block our healing by un-forgiveness and doubt.

YOUR DAILY REFLECTIONS

(Are you ready to take God at His Word today?)

(Write your response below.)

_____

_____

_____

_____

_____

_____

_____

_____

_____

_____

_____

DAY 2

PRAYER: (Use Sample Prayers or the ones you wrote from Day 1)

SCRIPTURE MEDITATION

Deuteronomy 30:19-20—(v.19)—I call heaven and earth to record this day against you; that I have set before you life and death, blessing and cursing: therefore choose life, that both thou and thy seed may live. (v.20) That thou mayest love the Lord thy God, and that thou mayest obey his voice, and that thou mayest cleave unto him: for he is thy life, and the length of thy days: that thou mayest dwell in the land which the Lord sware unto thy fathers, to Abraham, to Isaac, and to Jacob, to give them.

1 Kings 8:56—Blessed be the Lord that hath given rest unto his people Israel, according to all that he promised: there hath not failed one word of all his good promise, which he promised by the hand of Moses his servant.

DAILY DEVOTIONAL REFLECTIONS DAY 2

Choose Life

In Deut 30:19, God talks about putting the choice of life and death and blessing and cursing before us. He wants us to choose to be blessed even in times of pain, suffering or whatever we may be going through. We can receive His gift of blessing or be cursed for unbelief. We can choose life or death according to our faith. We should always pray the prayer of faith for God's healing and deliverance and believe God's Word no matter what things look like. The Lord loves us so much that He tells us to choose life because it is worth living with Jesus. Make sure you do not get caught up with your feelings or what you see, but choose life. I am so glad I chose life and life more abundantly. According to the Scriptures, God says He wishes that we prosper and be in health even as our souls prosper. (3 John 1:2)

YOUR DAILY REFLECTIONS

(Will you choose life today?)

_____
_____
_____
_____
_____
_____
_____
_____
_____
_____
_____
_____
_____

DAY 3

PRAYER

SCRIPTURE MEDITATION

Psalm 103:1-5 Bless the Lord, O my soul; and all that is within me. Bless his holy name. Bless the Lord, O my soul, and forget not all his benefits; Who redeemeth thy life from destruction; who crowneth thee with lovingkindness and tender mercies; Who satisfieth thy mouth with good things; so that thy youth is renewed like the eagle's.

Psalm 107:19-21 Then they cry unto the Lord in their trouble, and he saveth them out of their distresses. He sent his word, and healed them and delivered them from their destructions. Oh that men would praise the Lord for his goodness, and for his wonderful works to the children of men!

DAILY DEVOTIONAL REFLECTIONS DAY 3

Bless The Lord

Today, in Psalms 103: 1-5, we are being encouraged to bless the Lord with all our soul. It is so good to know that God has given us the power to bless Him as He blesses us. We have become partners with God in the blessing process. God is a great God and worthy to be praised! We are so glad God has healed all of our diseases and forgiven all of our sins. God wants us to praise Him for all His wonderful acts toward us. You should thank the Lord today for all of His loving kindness.

YOUR DAILY REFLECTIONS

(How can you bless the Lord today?)

_____

_____

_____

_____

_____

_____

_____

_____

_____

_____

_____

_____

_____

_____

_____

_____

_____

_____

DAY 4

PRAYER

SCRIPTURE MEDITATION

Psalm 118:16-17 The right hand of the Lord is exalted: the right hand of the Lord doeth valiantly. I shall not die, but live, and declare the works of the Lord.

Proverbs 4: 20-24 My son, attend to my words; incline thine ear unto my sayings. Let them not depart from thine eyes; keep them in the midst of thine heart. For they are life unto those that find them, and health to all their flesh. Keep thy heart with all diligence; for out of it are the issues of life. Put away from thee a froward mouth and perverse lips put far from thee.

DAILY DEVOTIONAL REFLECTIONS DAY 4

Power In The Word

As we read this Scripture today we focus on the power of the Word and why it is so important to read and meditate on the Word of God. The Word will not only direct our paths but cause health to come to our body, soul and spirit. We must believe in the Word to receive the strength to overcome the obstacles in our lives. Reciting Scriptures and declaring them over our lives will bring strength and power. Psalm 118:17, states that I will not die but live, and declare the works of the Lord. This is a powerful Scripture with promise. You must believe that God can keep you through sickness as well as any other problems you might be experiencing.

YOUR DAILY REFLECTIONS

(Have You Felt God's Power Today?)

_____
_____
_____
_____
_____
_____
_____
_____
_____
_____
_____
_____
_____
_____
_____
_____
_____
_____
_____
_____

DAY 5

PRAYER

SCRIPTURE MEDITATION

I saiah 41: 10 Fear thou not; for I am with thee: be not dismayed, for I am thy God; I will strengthen thee; yea I will help thee; yea, I will uphold thee with the right hand of my righteousness.

Isaiah 53:4-5 Surely he hath borne our griefs, and carried our sorrows: yet we did esteem him stricken, smitten of God, and afflicted. But he was wounded for our transgressions, he was bruised for our iniquities; the chastisement of our peace was upon him, and with his stripes we are healed.

Jeremiah 1: 12 Then said the Lord unto me. Thou hast well seen: for I will hasten my word to perform it.

DAILY DEVOTIONAL REFLECTIONS DAY 5

Fear Not

Today, our devotional thought surrounds the Scripture in Isaiah 41:10 which tells us not to fear, for God is with us in whatever circumstances we may find ourselves. These situations could be *physical, emotional, or spiritual.* God will always be there to uphold us with His righteousness and truth. We have to learn to rest in the Lord and wait patiently for His healing and deliverance. Sometimes we may feel that we are all alone in our situation but God is still there ready to help us. The Scripture says to wait patiently on God and He will strengthen your heart.

YOUR DAILY REFLECTIONS

(What are you fearing?)

_____

_____

_____

_____

_____

_____

_____

_____

_____

_____

_____

_____

_____

_____

_____

_____

_____

_____

DAY 6

PRAYER

SCRIPTURE MEDITATION

Jeremiah 30:17 For I will restore health unto thee, and I will heal thee of thy wounds, saith the Lord, because they called thee an Outcast, saying, This is Zion whom no man seeketh after.

Joel 3:10 Beat your plowshares into swords, and your pruning hooks into spears: let the weak say, I am strong.

Nahum 1:9 What do ye imagine against the Lord? He will make an utter end: affliction shall not rise up the second time.

Psalm 34:19 Many are the afflictions of the righteous: but the Lord delivereth him out of them all.

DAILY DEVOTIONAL REFLECTIONS DAY 6

Delivered From All Afflictions

God is speaking in the Scriptures above in a very forceful way saying He will deliver us out of all our afflictions because we are His righteous people. He will restore health unto us. He will heal all our wounds, no matter what they may be. He will make us whole *mentally, physically,* and *emotionally.* All we need to do is believe and live according to His Word. Keep looking up! Health and healing is on the way!

YOUR DAILY REFLECTIONS

(Is God delivering you yet?)

_____

_____

_____

_____

_____

_____

_____

_____

_____

_____

_____

_____

_____

_____

_____

_____

_____

_____

_____

DAY 7

PRAYER

SCRIPTURE MEDITATION

Matthew 8:2-3 And behold there came a leper and worshipped him, saying, Lord if thou wilt, thou canst make me clean. And Jesus put forth his hand, and touched him, saying, I will; be thou clean. And immediately his leprosy was cleansed.

Matthew 8:16-17 When the even was come, they brought unto him many that were possessed with devils: and he cast out the spirits with his word and healed all that were sick. That it might be fulfilled which was spoken by Esaias the prophet, saying, Himself took our infirmities and bare our sicknesses.

Matthew 18:18-19 Verily I say unto you, whatsoever ye shall bind on earth shall be bound in heaven: and whatsoever ye shall loose on earth shall loosed in heaven. Again I say unto you, That if two of you shall agree on earth as touching any thing that they shall ask, it shall be done for them of my Father which is in heaven.

DAILY DEVOTIONAL DAY 7

Does God Still Heal?

As we see in Matthew 8:2-3, the Lord is not concerned about the type of sickness we have; only that we believe that He can and *will heal us*. All God requires of us is to have faith in Him and His Word. Now you must exercise that faith by believing and God will do the rest. Be encouraged and stay strong through this trial. It's just *another "Test"* in life, because God already has the answer. But you must wait *patiently* for God to answer.

YOUR DAILY REFLECTIONS

(Do You Believe That God Will Heal You?)

_____
_____
_____
_____
_____
_____
_____
_____
_____
_____
_____
_____
_____
_____
_____
_____
_____
_____
_____

DAY 8

PRAYER:

SCRIPTURE MEDITATION

Matthew 21:21-22 Jesus answered and said unto them, Verily I say unto you. If ye have faith, and doubt not, ye shall not only do this which is done to the fig tree, but also if ye shall say unto this mountain, Be thou removed, and be thou cast unto the sea, it shall be done. And all things, whatsoever ye shall ask in prayer, believing, ye shall receive.

Mark 11: 22-24—And Jesus answering saith unto them, Have faith in God. For verily I say unto you that whosoever shall say unto this mountain, Be thou removed, and be thou cast unto the sea; and shall not doubt in his heart, but shall believe that those things which I said shall come to pass, he shall have whatsoever he saith. Therefore I say unto you, What things soever, ye desire, when ye pray believe ye receive them, and ye shall have them.

DAILY DEVOTIONAL REFLECTIONS DAY 8

We Must Believe By Faith

Sometimes as we read the Word of God we are challenged as in Matthew 21:21, where it states that we must believe by *faith* and do not doubt and we will do greater works. We can even say to the mountain be removed and be cast into the sea. This means that no matter how "big" the problem, with God we have the power to speak to the situation and it will go away or be resolved. Each day we must *exercise our faith* until we feel the strength and power to speak to the mountains in our lives and see God deliver us.

YOUR DAILY REFLECTIONS

(What mountains are you speaking to?)

_____

_____

_____

_____

_____

_____

_____

_____

_____

_____

_____

_____

_____

_____

_____

_____

_____

_____

DAY 9

SCRIPTURE MEDITATION

Mark 16: 14-18 Afterwards he appeared unto the eleven as they sat at meat, and upbraided them with their unbelief and hardness of heart, because they believed not them which had seen him after he was risen. And he said unto them, Go ye into all the world, and preach the gospel to every creature. He that believeth and is baptized shall be saved; but he that believeth not shall be damned. And these signs shall follow them that believe; In my name shall they cast out devils; they shall speak with new tongues; They shall take up serpents; and if they drink any deadly thing, it shall not hurt them, they shall lay hands on the sick, and they shall recover.

Romans 8:2 For the law of the Spirit of life in Christ Jesus hath made me free from the law of sin and death.

Romans 8:11 But if the Spirit of him that raised up Jesus from the dead dwell in you, he that raised up Christ from the dead shall also quicken your mortal bodies by his Spirit that dwelleth in you.

DAILY DEVOTIONAL REFLECTIONS DAY 9

Why Christ Died For Us

Let us not forget what Christ did during His ministry on earth (Mark 16:14-18). He *healed the sick, gave sight to the blind* and *raised the dead.* Even more important for us was what Christ did on the cross in *dying for our sins.* The Word also says by His stripes we are healed. We *must believe* that what God did for others he will do for *you and me.* In Romans 8:11 it states that if the same Spirit that raised Jesus from the dead dwells in us, then our bodies can be raised by that Spirit into health and wholeness. Activate your faith now, so the *healing power* of God will *flow* throughout your body today. God is waiting to *hear* from *you.*

YOUR DAILY REFLECTIONS

(What healing will you claim from the cross?)

_____

_____

_____

_____

_____

_____

_____

_____

_____

_____

DAY 10

PRAYER

SCRIPTURE MEDITATION

2 Corinthians 10:3-5 For through we walk in the flesh, we do not war after the flesh: For the weapons of our warfare are not carnal, but mighty through God to the pulling down of strong holds; Casting down imaginations, and every high thing that exalteth itself against the knowledge of God, and bringing into captivity every thought to the obedience of Christ.

Galatians 3:13-14 Christ hath redeemed us from the curse of the law, being made a curse for us: for it is written, Cursed is every one that hangeth on a tree: That the blessing of Abraham might come on the Gentiles through Jesus Christ; that we might receive the promise of the Spirit through faith.

Galatians 3:29 And if ye be Christ's, then are ye Abraham's seed, and heirs according to the promise.

DAILY DEVOTIONAL REFLECTIONS DAY 10

The Spiritual World Is Greater And More Powerful

Even though we live in a physical body, God speaks to us in 2 Cor.10:3-5, about a spiritual world that is *greater* and more *powerful*. In the spirit our weapons are *not physical* but *spiritual* and able to deliver us from all of the things that keep us in bondage. Such conditions as sickness, depression, anxiety and unbelief are just a few of these issues. We are told in the Word that we are heirs of the promise of blessed health through Jesus Christ. What an *awesome inheritance!*

YOUR DAILY REFLECTIONS

(How great is God in your life?)

_____

_____

_____

_____

_____

_____

_____

_____

_____

_____

_____

_____

_____

_____

_____

_____

_____

_____

_____

DAY 11

PRAYER

SCRIPTURE MEDITATION

Ephesians 6: 10-17 Finally, my brethren, be strong in the Lord, and in the power of his might. Put on the whole armour of God, that ye may be able to stand against the wiles of the devil. For we wrestle not against flesh and blood, but against principalities, against powers, against the rulers of the darkness of this world, against spiritual wickedness in high places. Wherefore take unto you the whole armour of God, that we may be able to withstand in the evil day and having done all, to stand. Stand therefore, having your loins girt about with truth, and having on the breastplate of righteousness; And your feet shod with the preparation of the gospel of peace; Above all, taking the shield of faith, wherewith ye shall be able to quench all the fiery darts of the wicked. And take the helmet of salvation, and the sword of the Spirit, which is the word of God:

DAILY DEVOTIONAL REFLECTIONS DAY 11

Stand And Be Strong In The Lord

In Ephesians 6:10-17, God is calling us to *stand* and *be strong* in the Lord. The situations of life we will have to face will come at us with great force from the enemy. Whether the situations are *physical sickness, mental depression, or spiritual issues,* only with God's power and might can we stand against the works of the enemy. We must remember that our fight is not against the people we see but against powers of darkness and spiritual wickedness in high places. We need to put on the *whole armour* of God if we are to stand. We also must have accepted Jesus Christ as our Lord and Savior and be walking in the Word and Spirit, if we are to receive this *peace and power.*

YOUR DAILY REFLECTIONS

(Do you have on the whole armour of God?)

_____
_____
_____
_____
_____
_____
_____
_____
_____
_____
_____
_____
_____
_____
_____
_____

DAY 12

PRAYER

SCRIPTURE MEDITATION

Philippians 2:13 For it is God which worketh in you both to will and to do of his good pleasure.

Philippians 4:6-7 Be careful for nothing: but in every thing by prayer and supplication with thanksgiving let your requests be made known unto God. And the peace of God, which passeth all understanding, shall keep your hearts and minds through Christ Jesus.

2 Timothy 1:7-For God hath not given us the spirit of fear; but of power, and of love, and of a sound mind.

Hebrews 10:23 Let us hold fast the profession of our faith without wavering: (for he is faithful that promised;)

DAILY DEVOTIONAL REFLECTIONS DAY 12

Worry Is Not Of God

In Philippians 4:6-7, we are told to pray about *everything* and submit our problems to God. Even when we are praying, we must begin to thank God for answered prayer. This is a requirement for receiving peace from God. But so many times we worry when we should be praying. I used to be what could be called a "professional worrier." I prayed but still worried even though in my heart I felt God would answer my prayers. I discovered through the Scriptures that worry is *unbelief* and causes us to doubt God, which is a *sin.* God is not a man, therefore, He does not lie. We also lose out on countless blessings from God because of unbelief. By faith we are healed and delivered and made whole by Christ Jesus. Live each day in belief and hope. In 2 Timothy 1:7, it states that God has not given us the spirit of fear but power, love and a sound mind.

YOUR DAILY REFLECTIONS

(Are you doubting God about something?)

_____

_____

_____

_____

_____

_____

_____

_____

_____

_____

DAY 13

PRAYER

SCRIPTURE MEDITATION

Hebrews 11:11 Through faith also Sara herself received strength to conceive seed, and was delivered of a child when she was past age, because she judged him faithful who had promised.

Hebrews 13:8 Jesus Christ the same yesterday, and to day, and for ever.

James 5:14-16 Is any sick among you? Let him call for the elders of the church; and let them pray over him, anointing him with oil in the name of the Lord: And the prayer of faith shall save the sick, and the Lord shall raise him up; and if he have committed sins, they shall be forgiven him. Confess your faults one to another, and pray one for another, that ye may be healed. The effectual fervent prayer of a righteous man availeth much.

DAILY DEVOTIONAL REFLECTIONS DAY 13

Faith Is The Key In Healing

We learn today in James 5:14-16 that having faith is the *key element* in receiving healing from God. The Scriptures also tell us when you are sick how you are to call on the elders of the church to pray and anoint you with oil. Another requirement needed in total healing is to confess our sins and pray for one another that we can be healed. James 5:16 states that " . . . . the effectual fervent prayer of a righteous man availeth much." Make sure you have confessed all sins so that nothing is blocking your relationship with the Lord.

YOUR DAILY REFLECTIONS

(Have you called the elders to pray and anoint you with oil?)

_____

_____

_____

_____

_____

_____

_____

_____

_____

_____

_____

_____

_____

_____

_____

_____

_____

_____

DAY 14

PRAYER

SCRIPTURE MEDITATION

1 Peter 2:24 Who his own self bare our sins in his own body on the tree, that we, being dead to sins, should live unto righteousness: by whose stripes ye were healed.

1 John 3:21-22 Beloved, if our heart condemn us not, then have we confidence toward God. And whatsoever we ask, we receive of him, because we keep his commandments, and do those things that are pleasing in his sight.

1 John 5:14-15 And this is the confidence that we have in him, that, if we ask anything according to his will, he heareth us: And if we know that he hear us, whatsoever we ask, we know that we have the petitions that we desired of him.

3 John 1:2—Beloved I wish above all things that thou mayest prosper and be in health, even as thy soul prospereth.

DAILY DEVOTIONAL REFLECTIONS DAY 14

Ask, Believe And Receive

Today, we find in our Scriptures several key words which are "ask," "believe," and "receive." These are *powerful words* with promise! God will give to us what we ask. In 1 John 5:14-15 it says that we must ask *according to God's will* and He will hear us. This is why we must ask first of all for forgiveness of our sins and then we will be in line to ask anything. We can ask for healing and deliverance from whatever has us bound, and God will answer our prayers. We must believe without doubting what the Word says if we want to receive it. Remember, according to 3 John 1:2, that God's wish is that we should prosper and be in good health even as our soul prospers.

YOUR DAILY REFLECTIONS

(What have you asked and believed God for today?)

_____

_____

_____

_____

_____

_____

_____

_____

_____

_____

_____

_____

_____

_____

_____

_____

DAY 15

PRAYER

SCRIPTURE MEDITATION

Matthew 9:35 And Jesus went about all the cities and villages, teaching in their synagogues, and preaching the gospel of the kingdom, and healing every sickness and every disease among the people.

Luke 9:10-11 And the apostles, when they were returned, told him all that they had done. And he took them, and went aside privately into a desert place belonging to the city called Bethsaida. And the people, when they knew it, followed him: and he received them, and spake unto them of the kingdom of God, and healed them that had need of healing.

Romans 10:9-10—That if thou shalt *confess* with thy *mouth* the *Lord Jesus,* and shalt *believe in thine heart* that *God* hath *raised him* from the *dead, thou* shalt be *saved.* For with the *heart* man *believeth* unto *righteousness;* and with the *mouth confession* is made unto *salvation.*

Revelation 12:11 And they overcame him by the blood of the Lamb, and by the word of their testimony; and they loved not their lives unto the death.

DAILY DEVOTIONAL REFLECTIONS DAY 15

Jesus: Master, Teacher, Preacher And Healer

As we are told from the Scripture in Matthew 9:35, Jesus went all over *teaching, preaching* and *healing* people of every sickness and disease. But, we find that the *greatest healing* we can receive is the one for *our souls*. In Romans 10:9-10, it says that if we confess our sins and believe in our hearts that God has raised Jesus from the dead we will be saved. What a joy to know that we have eternal life not only here on earth but in heaven. God desires not only our bodies to be healed but our souls as well. We give praise to God for His marvelous works in our lives! If you have not received Jesus Christ in your life the best time is *now.*

YOUR DAILY REFLECTIONS

(Have you believed God's report for your life?)

_____

_____

_____

_____

_____

_____

_____

_____

If you still feel you need more time in the Word, repeat these devotionals for another 15 days.

CLAIMING HEALING
AS A WAY OF LIFE

After completing the *fifteen or thirty day Spiritual Journey,* you will begin to feel God's presence even more in your life. You will sense a greater awareness of God's power as you *pray* and *read His Word.* Your spirit will be more open to hearing God's voice and following His will. You will begin to experience a hunger and thirst for God's Word daily. If you miss your daily devotional time with God you will begin to *feel weak* in your *spirit.* This is a *sign* that tells you that you are *growing in your relationship* with the Lord. As you continue to meditate on God's Word, you will begin to seek wisdom from the Scriptures rather than from friends or your own thinking. One thing for sure *is you will never be the same* after you have experienced God's presence through this spiritual journey.

You should *use* these *Scriptures* as a *daily source* of *strength* for yourself and others who might be ill, physically, spiritually or emotionally. I have used these Scriptures over the last seven years and have seen God do miracles in people's lives through His Word. Every time I would minister with the Scriptures or give them to family, friends or someone who was ill, I would feel God urging me to finish this book. I also felt led to finish this book because there have been many who commented on how they were encouraged in their faith by the Scripture readings.

On numerous occasions I was asked when will the book be completed. I always had so many excuses because of the time restraints of ministry and family, but God let me know that it was time to fulfill my destiny. I had to use the Word to give me strength to fight off the forces that were trying to keep me from doing God's will by writing this book. I had to start setting aside periods of time to meet with God and allow Him to give me a plan. As I meditated on the Word, God gave me a plan. It included spending time working on the book every day no matter how much time I had to spend. Each day is a new struggle, but we must fight if we are to receive the prize that God has for us. Now that you have completed the prayer and Scripture reading journey, take the next step and begin to work on the questions in the workbook. Take time to go back over your daily reflections as you respond to each question.

SCRIPTURAL HEALING

WORKBOOK

SCRIPTURAL HEALING WORKBOOK

(For personal or group study)

(Please complete to receive a greater insight into Scriptural healing)

1.   How did you feel after reading your daily Scriptures?

_____
_____
_____
_____
_____
_____
_____

2.   What promise(s) in each Scripture did God make to you?

_____
_____
_____
_____
_____
_____
_____

3. Now write a "Thank You" note to God for His promise (s).

_____
_____
_____
_____
_____
_____
_____

4. When did you first begin to feel healing occur in your body, mind, and spirit?

_____
_____
_____
_____
_____
_____

5. What did the healing or deliverance feel like? Describe your feeling in 10 words or less.

_____
_____
_____
_____
_____
_____
_____
_____
_____
_____
_____
_____

6. In your daily reading, what verse(s) helped you the most?

_____

_____

_____

_____

_____

_____

7. Thank God again for the process of healing by faith.

_____

_____

_____

_____

_____

_____

8. What are some characteristics of the people who have been healed or delivered in your Scripture reading?

_____

_____

_____

_____

_____

_____

_____

_____

_____

_____

_____

_____

_____

9. *What did they need God to do for them?*

_____
_____
_____
_____
_____
_____
_____

10. *Do you think your situation or problem is greater than those in the Bible?*

   Yes____ or No_____ Please explain:

_____
_____
_____
_____
_____
_____

11. *Compare your need for healing or deliverance with theirs. Is your need greater or lesser? Please explain:*

_____
_____
_____
_____
_____
_____
_____
_____
_____
_____

12. *Give thanks for what God is doing in your life by writing your thoughts.*

_____

_____

_____

_____

_____

_____

_____

13. *Chart your spiritual growth so far on a scale of one to ten. Where do you see your growth in faith by reading and meditating on the Word? Please circle the number that represents how you feel so far.*

(lesser) (1—2—3—4—5—6—7—8—9—10) (greater)

14. *Is your score six or less? Yes___ or No___ If yes, then you should repeat the 15-Day Scripture reading devotions at least one or two times until you feel God's strength and the power of His healing.*

____I will repeat the daily Scriptures to grow stronger.
____I do not need to repeat them at this time.

15. *If you have spent another 15-Days in Scripture, prayer and praise I am sure you feel better. No matter how much time it takes let the Lord totally heal and deliver you. Be sure to chart your spiritual growth again.*

(lesser) (1—2—3—4—5—6—7—8—9—10) (greater)

SCRIPTURAL
HEALING WORKBOOK NOTES

_____
_____
_____
_____
_____
_____
_____
_____
_____
_____
_____
_____
_____
_____
_____
_____

PRAYER JOURNAL NOTES

Edwards Brothers Malloy
Thorofare, NJ USA
April 15, 2014